Cooperation

Kimberley Jane Pryor

MACMILLAN
LIBRARY

First published in 2008 by
MACMILLAN EDUCATION AUSTRALIA PTY LTD
15–19 Claremont Street, South Yarra 3141

Visit our website at www.macmillan.com.au or go directly to www.macmillanlibrary.com.au

Associated companies and representatives throughout the world.

National Library of Australia
Cataloguing-in-Publication data

Pryor, Kimberley Jane, 1962– .
 Cooperation.

 Includes index.
 For primary school age.
 ISBN 978 1 4202 1871 8 (hbk.).

 1. Values – Juvenile literature. 2. Cooperation – Juvenile
 literature. I. Title. (Series: MYL values).

179.9

Edited by Helena Newton
Text and cover design by Christine Deering
Page layout by Raul Diche and Domenic Lauricella
Photo research by Naomi Parker and Legend Images

Printed in China

Acknowledgements

The author and the publisher are grateful to the following for permission to reproduce copyright material:

Front cover photograph of friends building a sandcastle courtesy of Photos.com

Photos courtesy of:
Corbis RF, **25**; Digital Vision/Getty Images, **17, 26**; Photodisc/Getty Images, **15**; iStockphoto.com, **3, 11**;
© Ana Abejon/iStockphoto.com, **24**; © arpiaphoto.com/iStockphoto.com, **5**; © arturbo/iStockphoto.com, **18**;
© Ronald Bloom/iStockphoto.com, **20**; © geotrac/iStockphoto.com, **29**; © bonnie jacobs/iStockphoto.com, **8,
12**; © Tomaz Levstek/iStockphoto.com, **30**; © Sean Locke/iStockphoto.com, **14, 16**; © marmion/iStockphoto.
com, **9**; © Carmen Martinez Banús/iStockphoto.com, **10**; © Christopher Pattberg/iStockphoto.com, **28**; © Josef
Philipp/iStockphoto.com, **19**; © Julián Rovagnati/iStockphoto.com, **21**; © Marzanna Syncerz/iStockphoto.com, **4**;
Photodisc, **13, 23**; Photos.com, **1, 6**; Stockbyte, **27**; Stockdisc, **7**; Thinkstock Royalty-Free, **22**.

While every care has been taken to trace and acknowledge copyright, the publisher tenders their apologies for
any accidental infringement where copyright has proved untraceable. Where the attempt has been unsuccessful,
the publisher welcomes information that would redress the situation.

For Nick, Ashley and Thomas

Contents

Glossary words

When a word is printed in **bold**, you can look up its meaning in the Glossary on page 31.

Values

Values are the things you believe in. They guide the way:

- you think

- you speak

- you **behave**.

Values help you to play happily with friends in a pool.

Values help you to decide what is right and what is wrong. They also help you to live your life in a meaningful way.

Values help you to follow the rules when playing hide-and-seek.

Cooperation

Cooperation is working together. It is teaming up with another person or other people to do or make something.

Friends often work together to build sandcastles.

Cooperation is also being helpful. It is giving **assistance** to people when they need it.

It is helpful to show someone how to use a new computer program.

Cooperative people

Cooperative people are **willing** to do what others ask them to do. They follow the **instructions** given for an activity or job.

Cooperative students listen carefully and follow their teacher's instructions.

Cooperative people find ways to **solve problems**. They try to get on well with their family, friends and neighbours.

Cooperative neighbours talk to one another about community problems.

Cooperating with family

In a family, people cooperate by being kind to each other. They listen to each other and help each other out.

It is kind to help your younger sister learn to read and write.

Family members cooperate by sharing the jobs around the house. Some jobs are done more easily when two or more people work together.

This brother and sister work together to rake the lawn.

Cooperating with friends

Friends cooperate when they work together. When friends work on school projects together, they listen to each other's ideas. They also share the work.

It is fun to work on a project with a friend.

Friends also cooperate when they play together.
They share toys and take turns at the playground.

Letting
everyone have
a turn on the
swing shows
cooperation.

Cooperating with neighbours

Cooperative people are **thoughtful** towards their neighbours. They do not make loud noises that might disturb their neighbours.

It is thoughtful to write to your neighbours if you are planning a large party.

Neighbours often cooperate by taking care of things in their neighbourhood. Sometimes they work together to clean and fix their local school or community hall.

Sometimes neighbours work together to plant a community garden.

Ways to cooperate

There are many different ways to cooperate with your family, friends and neighbours. Following instructions is a good way to start being cooperative.

You can learn how to break an egg when you follow instructions.

Doing an activity with a partner is another way to practise cooperation. Being helpful is also a part of being cooperative.

Partners need to cooperate when they run together in a three-legged race.

Following instructions

Following instructions is one way to cooperate with others. You can learn new things when you follow the instructions of family members or teachers.

Following your swimming teacher's instructions helps you learn to swim.

Written instructions can tell you how to play a game or put a toy together. They can also tell you how to use the toy properly and safely.

Following written instructions with someone else can help you to practise cooperation.

Sharing

Sharing is another way to cooperate with others. Some people are very good at sharing. They share their favourite toys with their friends.

It is kind to bring your favourite ball to the park to share with friends.

Brothers and sisters need to cooperate when they share a bedroom. They need to work together to keep the bedroom clean and tidy.

Brothers and sisters sometimes enjoy sharing books.

Working with others

Many people find that they do better work when they work with others. A group of people working together can get a job done more quickly.

These people are enjoying working together.

When they work together, people can teach each other new **skills**. They can also learn new skills from each other.

Students share their skills when they paint a mural together.

Being in a team

People often need to work as part of a team. In a sports team, players cooperate by following the rules of the game.

Soccer players cooperate by doing what their coach asks.

Players also cooperate by making sure that everyone gets a turn. When they take their turn, they do their best so that the team does well.

All the members of a basketball team need to work together.

Helping others

Cooperative people like helping others. If they see a person in need, they offer to help.

Helping a family member to search for a lost toy is cooperative.

Cooperative people help when someone asks them to help. They also ask for help when they need it.

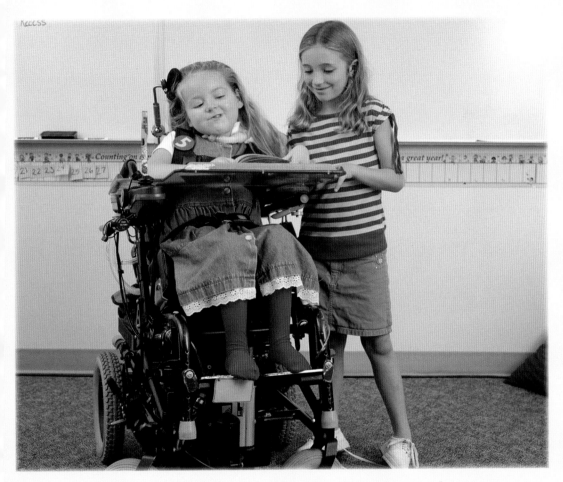

You can help a classmate by turning the pages of a book while she reads.

Solving problems

Solving problems is part of cooperation. Cooperative people think of different ways to solve a problem. Then they choose one way and try it.

Brainstorming is thinking of lots of different ways to solve a problem.

Cooperative people do not shout or hurt others when they feel angry. They calm down and think before they say or do anything. This helps them to solve problems.

Taking a deep breath or counting to ten helps people to calm down when they are angry.

Personal set of values

There are many different values. Everyone has a personal set of values. This set of values guides people in big and little ways in their daily lives.

Cooperation is an important value for building workers to have.

Glossary

assistance   a helping hand

behave   act in a certain way

instructions   words that tell you how to do something or how to behave

problems   things that are difficult to understand or do

skills   abilities that help you to do activities or jobs well

solve   find the answer to

thoughtful   showing that you think and care about others

willing   happy and ready to help

Index